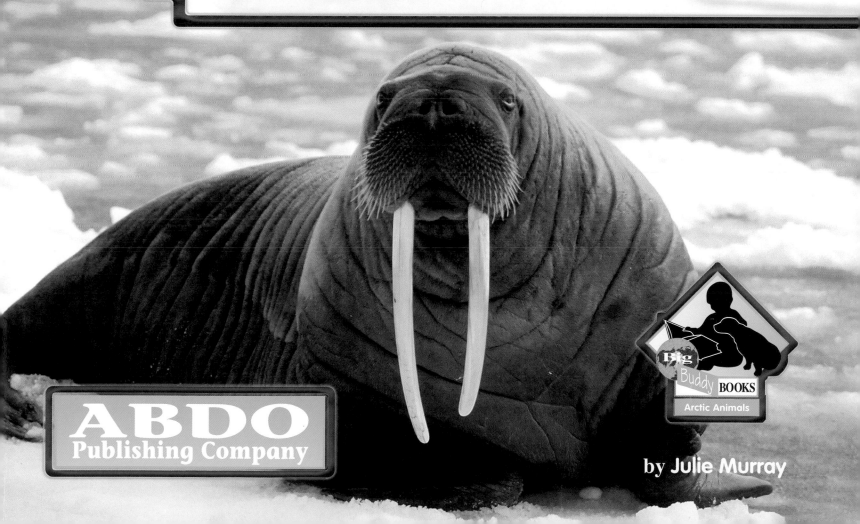

Arctic Animals

Walruses

ABDO
Publishing Company

Big Buddy BOOKS
Arctic Animals

by Julie Murray

VISIT US AT
www.abdopublishing.com

Published by ABDO Publishing Company, PO Box 398166, Minneapolis, Minnesota 55439.

Copyright © 2014 by Abdo Consulting Group, Inc. International copyrights reserved in all countries. No part of this book may be reproduced in any form without written permission from the publisher. Big Buddy Books™ is a trademark and logo of ABDO Publishing Company.

Printed in the United States of America, North Mankato, Minnesota.
032013
092013

 PRINTED ON RECYCLED PAPER

Coordinating Series Editor: Rochelle Baltzer
Editor: Marcia Zappa
Contributing Editors: Megan M. Gunderson, Sarah Tieck
Graphic Design: Maria Hosley
Cover Photograph: *Getty Images*: Steven Kazlowski.
Interior Photographs/Illustrations: *Getty Images*: Mark Carwardine (p. 11), Sue Flood (p. 8), Steven Kazlowski (p. 7), Paul Nicklen (p. 25), Norbert Rosing (p. 27), Rodney Ungwiluk, Jr. Photography (p. 23); *Glow Images*: © W. Perry Conway/CORBIS (p. 13), Paul Souders (p. 15), SuperStock (p. 9); *iStockphoto*: ©iStockphoto.com/ekvals (p. 17), ©iStockphoto.com/JohnPitcher (p. 9), ©iStockphoto.com/wdj (p. 20); *National Geographic Stock*: Martha Cooper (p. 14), Paul Nicklen (p. 17); *Photo Researchers, Inc.*: Bryan and Cherry Alexander (p. 27); *Shutterstock*: Hal Brindley (p. 19), Matthew Jacques (p. 4), Vladimir Melnik (pp. 5, 11), outdoorsman (p. 29), Christopher Wood (p. 4).

Library of Congress Cataloging-in-Publication Data

Murray, Julie, 1969-
  Walruses / Julie Murray.
    p. cm. -- (Arctic animals)
  Audience: 7-11.
  ISBN 978-1-61783-802-6
  1. Walrus--Juvenile literature. 2. Walrus--Behavior--Juvenile literature. I. Title.
  QL737.P62M87 2014
  599.79'9--dc23
                    2012049648

Contents

Earth has many different **regions**. But, few stand out as much as the Arctic. This is the northernmost part of Earth. The area is known for its freezing cold weather and great sheets of ice.

Walruses are large sea animals. They are known for their long, ivory teeth called tusks.

The Arctic includes land from several **continents**. It also includes the Arctic Ocean and the huge sea of ice that floats on it. The Arctic is home to many interesting animals. One of these is the walrus.

Walrus Territory

There are two main types of walruses. Atlantic walruses live along the coasts of Greenland and northeastern Canada. Pacific walruses live along the coasts of Russia and Alaska.

Walruses spend much of their lives in shallow seas. They rest out of the water on snow-covered sea ice. They also rest on sandy or rocky islands and shores.

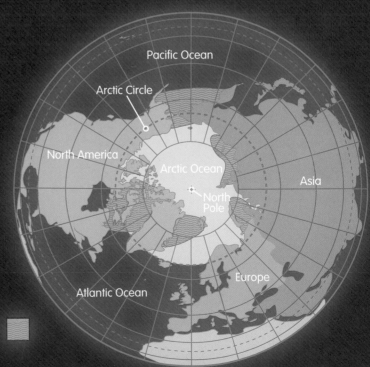

Pacific Ocean

Arctic Circle

North America

Arctic Ocean

Asia

North Pole

Europe

Atlantic Ocean

Walrus Territory

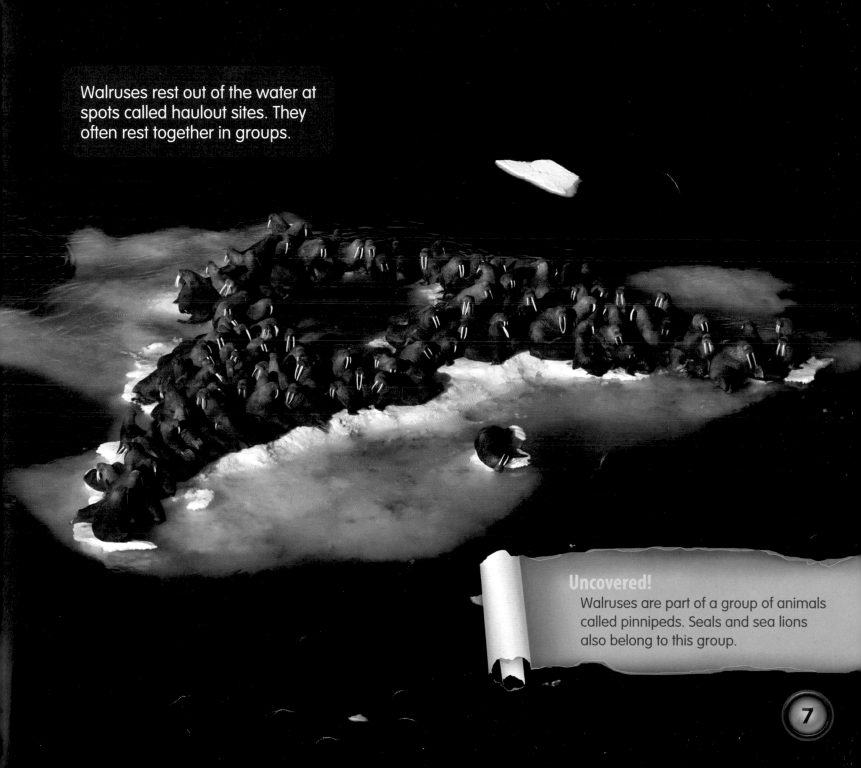

Walruses rest out of the water at spots called haulout sites. They often rest together in groups.

Uncovered!
Walruses are part of a group of animals called pinnipeds. Seals and sea lions also belong to this group.

Welcome to the Arctic!

If you took a trip to where walruses live, you might find...

...Inuit people.

The Inuit of North America were among the first people to live in the Arctic. They hunted walruses for meat. They used the skin to make shelters and boats. And, they burned oil from walrus fat for heat and light. Today, the Inuit are among the few people still allowed to hunt walruses in North America.

Gulf of Alaska

BEAUFORT SEA

GREENLAND

(Kalaallit Nunaat)

GREENLAND SEA

NORWEGIAN SEA

Bering
Strait

EAST SIBERIAN
SEA

CHUKCHI SEA

LAPTEV SEA

TIC OCEAN

← North Pole

KARA

...islands.

Many islands dot the Arctic Ocean. Greenland is a large island that belongs to Denmark. Greenland includes ATOW1996, which is one of the northernmost islands on Earth. Iceland is an island country just south of the Arctic Circle. And, Canada has many islands in the Arctic Ocean.

...wild weather.

The Arctic is known for its freezing cold winters. It can be as cold as -76°F (-60°C)! But, the Arctic has warm weather too. During the summer, it can be as warm as 86°F (30°C)! Walruses generally live where the temperature is 5° to 41°F (-15° to 5°C).

9

Take a Closer Look

Walruses have long, rounded bodies. They have four small, flat flippers. A walrus has small eyes on the sides of its head. Its short **snout** has thick whiskers.

Walruses are large animals. Adults are 7 to 12 feet (2 to 4 m) long. They weigh 880 to 3,700 pounds (400 to 1,700 kg). Females are smaller than males.

A walrus has a layer of fat under its skin. This fat is called blubber. It can be up to four inches (10 cm) thick! Blubber helps trap heat inside a walrus's body.

Adult walruses are gray or dark, reddish brown. Their bodies are covered in short, thin hair. But, their flippers are bare.

Walruses have thick, wrinkled skin. This guards against rough rocks, sharp ice, and the tusks of other walruses.

Uncovered!
During winter, blubber can make up one-third of a walrus's body mass!

Useful Tusks

Walruses are known for their large tusks. Both males and females have tusks. But, the tusks of males are larger. They can grow more than three feet (1 m) long!

Walruses have many uses for their tusks. They use them as hooks to pull their large bodies out of the water. They use them to break breathing holes in ice. And, they use them to fight predators and each other.

Uncovered!
Walruses have few natural predators. But, killer whales sometimes attack them. And, polar bears sometimes hunt walrus babies.

A walrus's tusks grow for about 15 years.

Water World

Walruses spend about two-thirds of their lives in water. They are well built for swimming. They use their square-shaped front flippers to change direction. They paddle with their triangle-shaped back flippers.

Walruses can swim more than 20 miles (30 km) per hour for short lengths. But, they usually swim much slower.

On land, walruses turn their front flippers outward. They turn their back flippers forward. Then, they are able to walk on all fours.

Walruses usually stay in shallow water. They can be underwater for up to ten minutes!

Mealtime

Walruses are carnivores. That means they eat meat. Walruses eat clams, mussels, shrimps, worms, and some slow-moving fish. These types of animals live on or near the ocean floor. There, it is often dark. So, walruses feel with their whiskers to find food.

When a walrus finds food, it sucks it into its mouth. Sometimes, food is buried on the ocean floor. So, a walrus spits a jet of water to uncover it. Or, it uses its front flippers to wave away sand and mud.

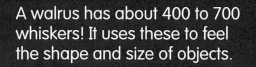

A walrus has about 400 to 700 whiskers! It uses these to feel the shape and size of objects.

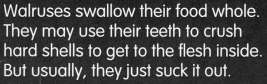

Walruses swallow their food whole. They may use their teeth to crush hard shells to get to the flesh inside. But usually, they just suck it out.

Uncovered!

Walruses are very large compared to the animals they eat. So, they eat a lot to survive. An adult walrus can eat more than 3,000 clams in one feeding!

Social Life

Walruses are **social** animals. They spend much of their time in groups called herds. Males and females form separate herds.

Each walrus herd has a leader. The leader is usually the largest walrus with the largest tusks. Herd leaders get the best spots at haulout sites.

Uncovered!
Walrus herds are often large. They may have thousands of members!

At haulout sites, herd members lie close together. Sometimes, they even lie on top of one another.

Sometimes, another large walrus **challenges** a herd leader. Usually, the leader uses body language to scare it away. But, sometimes they fight.

Walruses fight by slashing each other with their tusks. Fights are most common between males during the **mating** season, from January through April.

Walruses are loud animals. They make many noises above and below water to share their feelings. These include snorts, grunts, growls, barks, whistles, and clicks.

Moving Along

Most walruses **migrate** to stay near the southern edge of Arctic sea ice. During winter, they move south. During summer, they move north.

Some walruses migrate more than 1,800 miles (2,900 km) each year. They mostly travel by swimming. But sometimes, they ride on floating chunks of ice.

Uncovered!

Scientists believe female Pacific walruses and their young migrate the farthest. Other walruses are less likely to travel as far.

Female Pacific walruses give birth during their northern migration.

Baby Walruses

Uncovered!
A walrus mother works very hard to keep her calf safe. She often shelters it under her chest between her front flippers.

Walruses are **mammals**. Females usually have one baby at a time. They give birth on land or sea ice.

Baby walruses are called calves. At birth, a calf weighs 100 to 165 pounds (45 to 75 kg). It drinks its mother's milk and grows.

Baby walruses are grayish brown and have short, soft fur. Their skin changes as they grow.

A walrus calf can swim right after being born. But, it takes about a month for it to swim well. A calf follows its mother while she searches for food. It can drink milk on land or underwater.

After about six months, a walrus calf starts eating food. It stops drinking milk after about two years. A calf usually leaves its mother at this time. But if its mother is not expecting a new baby, it may stay longer.

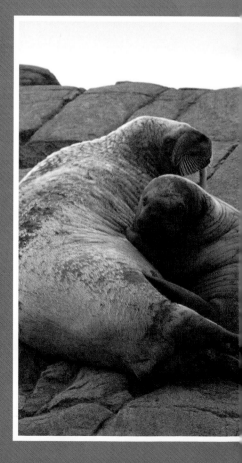

A walrus calf often rides on its mother's back.

Walrus mothers with calves often form their own herds. These are called nursery herds.

Survivors

Life in the Arctic isn't easy for walruses. Long ago, people commonly hunted them. **Pollution** and businesses such as shipping harm their **habitat**. And, **global warming** is melting Arctic sea ice. Walruses rest and give birth on this ice.

Still, walruses **survive**. There are laws that limit hunting them. And, people work to make sure they have large, clean places to live freely. Walruses help make the Arctic an amazing place.

In the wild, walruses live for up to 40 years.

Wow!
I'll bet you never knew...

...that walruses go bald. As they get older, their hair gets thinner. Male walruses especially lose hair around their necks and chests.

...that the walrus's Latin name, *Odobenus rosmarus*, means "tooth-walking sea-horse." And, the word *walrus* comes from the Danish word for "sea horse."

...that walruses have tails. But, you usually can't see a walrus's tail. That's because it is hidden under a fold of skin.

...that a walrus's skin changes color when it is in cold water. There, it becomes very light gray. This is because less blood is flowing near the skin. This helps a walrus stay warm.

Important Words

challenge (CHA-luhnj) to test one's strengths or abilities.

continent one of Earth's seven main land areas.

global warming an increase in the average temperature of Earth's surface.

habitat a place where a living thing is naturally found.

mammal a member of a group of living beings. Mammals make milk to feed their babies and usually have hair or fur on their skin.

mate to join as a couple in order to reproduce, or have babies.

migrate to move from one place to another to find food or have babies.

pollution human waste that dirties or harms air, water, or land.

region a large part of the world that is different from other parts.

snout a part of the face, including the nose and the mouth, that sticks out. Some animals, such as walruses, have a snout.

social (SOH-shuhl) naturally living or growing in groups.

survive to continue to live or exist.

Web Sites

To learn more about walruses, visit ABDO Publishing Company online. Web sites about walruses are featured on our Book Links page. These links are routinely monitored and updated to provide the most current information available.

www.abdopublishing.com

Index